Animals in My Yard

Raccoons

by Amy McDonald

BLASTOFF! Beginners

BELLWETHER MEDIA
MINNEAPOLIS, MN

 **Blastoff! Beginners** are developed by literacy experts and educators to meet the needs of early readers. These engaging informational texts support young children as they begin reading about their world. Through simple language and high frequency words paired with crisp, colorful photos, Blastoff! Beginners launch young readers into the universe of independent reading.

Sight Words in This Book

a	but	from	people	they
all	by	good	see	too
and	day	have	some	you
are	eat	help	their	
at	find	I	them	
black	for	in	these	

This edition first published in 2021 by Bellwether Media, Inc.

No part of this publication may be reproduced in whole or in part without written permission of the publisher. For information regarding permission, write to Bellwether Media, Inc., Attention: Permissions Department, 6012 Blue Circle Drive, Minnetonka, MN 55343.

Library of Congress Cataloging-in-Publication Data

Names: McDonald, Amy, author.
Title: Raccoons / by Amy McDonald.
Description: Minneapolis, MN : Bellwether Media, 2021. | Series: Animals in my yard | Includes bibliographical references and index. | Audience: Grades PreK-2
Identifiers: LCCN 2020007071 (print) | LCCN 2020007072 (ebook) | ISBN 9781644873106 (library binding) | ISBN 9781681037974 (paperback) | ISBN 9781681037738 (ebook)
Subjects: LCSH: Raccoon--Juvenile literature.
Classification: LCC QL737.C26 M427 2021 (print) | LCC QL737.C26 (ebook) | DDC 599.76/32--dc23
LC record available at https://lccn.loc.gov/2020007071
LC ebook record available at https://lccn.loc.gov/2020007072

Text copyright © 2021 by Bellwether Media, Inc. BLASTOFF! BEGINNERS and associated logos are trademarks and/or registered trademarks of Bellwether Media, Inc.

Editor: Christina Leaf   Designer: Jeffrey Kollock

Printed in the United States of America, North Mankato, MN.

Table of Contents

Raccoons!	4
Body Parts	6
The Lives of Raccoons	12
Raccoon Facts	22
Glossary	23
To Learn More	24
Index	24

Raccoons!

You have a mask but I see you! Hello, raccoon!

Body Parts

Raccoons have black masks. These help them see at night.

Raccoons have sharp teeth. These help them hunt.

Raccoons have hands. They grab and hold things.

The Lives of Raccoons

Raccoons live in **dens**. Some live by people.

Raccoons sleep at home all day. They find food at night.

Raccoons eat plants, rats, and fish. They eat trash, too!

plants

Raccoons are **clever**. They work hard for food.

Cubs learn from their mom. Good job, cub!

cubs

Raccoon Facts

Raccoon Body Parts

mask

teeth

hands

Raccoon Food

plants

fish

trash

Glossary

clever

smart and skilled

cubs

baby raccoons

dens

homes built by animals

To Learn More

ON THE WEB

FACTSURFER

Factsurfer.com gives you a safe, fun way to find more information.

1. Go to www.factsurfer.com.

2. Enter "raccoons" into the search box and click 🔍.

3. Select your book cover to see a list of related content.

Index

clever, 18
cubs, 20
day, 14
dens, 12, 13
fish, 16, 17
food, 14, 18
hands, 10, 11
hunt, 8
learn, 20

mask, 4, 6, 7
mom, 20
night, 6, 14
people, 12
plants, 16
rats, 16, 17
sleep, 14
teeth, 8, 9
trash, 16, 17

The images in this book are reproduced through the courtesy of: Eric Isselee, front cover, pp. 3, 22 (isolated); Sonsedska Yuliia, pp. 4, 5; Becky Sheridan, pp. 6-7; Edwin Butter, pp. 8-9; Debbie Steinhausser, p. 10; Stan Tekiela, pp. 10-11; Figtography, pp. 12-13; Kuttig - Animals/ Alamy, pp. 14-15; Magalie St-Hilaire poulin, pp. 16-17; Mazur Travel, p. 16; Gallinago_media, p. 17 (rats); feathercollector, p. 17 (fish); Martin Smart/ Alamy, pp. 18-19; Agnieszka Bacal, p. 20; L-N, pp. 20-21; Landshark1, p. 22 (plants); Susy Baels, p. 22 (fish); Will Rodrigues, p. 22 (trash); The Old Major, p. 23 (clever); Geoffrey Kuchera, p. 23 (cubs); 13Smile, p. 23 (dens).